Lute and Scimitar

LUTE

AND

SCIMITAR

being Poems and Ballads of Central Asia trans-
lated out of the Afghan, the Persian, the Turk-
oman, the Tarantchi, the Bokharan, the
Balochi, and the Tartar tongues together
with an Introduction and Historical
and Philological Annotations

by

ACHMED ABDULLAH

AND WITH A PREFACE BY

HERVEY ALLEN

WILDSIDE PRESS

WILDSIDE PRESS

To

My Friend

Henry Wysham Lanier

Preface

by

Hervey Allen

THERE is a great belt of land across Central Asia, stretching roughly from the Himalayas to the plains of Hungary in Europe, that for time out of mind has been the open road, the camping place, and the abode of restless and powerful peoples. Here in the dim antraes of the past one catches the misty pageantry of race migrations: the Yellow Man presses west or the White Man thrusts eastward. Along its grassy steppes before the dawn of history the Celts drifted into Europe, leaving behind them here and there strange enclaves where forgotten dialects of the ancient Celtic tongues heard by Caesar in Gaul and Britain still flourish in the dizzy gorges of the Caucasus. These memorials of a passing of peoples distant in time are so persistent that the conventions of form in literature, root words, phrases, and the social attitudes in song and story which they embalm are in many instances still similar in places so far apart as Afghanistan, the west coast of Ireland, and the Scottish Highlands. If, in these translations, the reader is therefore occasionally startled by a familiar twist of phrase or characteristic attitude it will not be by accident alone.

But the passing of the Celts is only one of many migrations to be recorded. Along the same road also passed the Aryans, still a pastoral people, drifting westward. Then came waves of Yellow Men on stocky little horses, moving slowly, horde after horde, out of their great homeland in upper Mongolia which slowly grew drier as the seismic forces raised it higher and higher, until its inhabitants driven by the urge that drives all men, sought subsistence for their flocks and herds elsewhere in pastures ever new.

Through this colorful and ever-changing warp of empires and peoples stretching east and west from Thibet to Iran, shot ever fitfully the woof of invasions from the north and south: Greeks

7

and Slavs from the north and westward, Chinese and Indians, yellow and dark-faced peoples from the east and south. Twenty-three centuries ago Alexander clove his way across it, leaving a faint silver streak of Greek cities and culture, impressing his two-horned, godlike head on ancient coins that may still be found occasionally in the dower bangles of slant-eyed maidens, pressing the memory of the face of Apollo upon the lineaments of Bactrian Buddhas where it still glimmers faintly, and leaving the hardy ghost of his name, "Iskander," upon which to drape many an heroic tale. His, indeed, is still a legend so potent that to this day Iskander remains one of the favorite names for Afghan boys.

For this Central Asian "road," this path between the East and West, has forever haunted the dreams of conquerors. Caesar was planning to set out upon it when the conspirators stopped him. From it the Roman eagles turned back under Trajan. Napoleon dreamed of taking it to India while fighting the Mamelukes under the pyramids, and its more modern possibilities continue to trouble and to intrigue both Downing Street and Moscow. It is still the great borderland par excellence, the political, social, and religious debatable ground of the world.

Yet all the peoples who followed this the greatest of trails did not merely pass. Some of them, or part of them, settled down in some country which took their fancy or that their necessity required. Thus remnants of tribe or nation thrust themselves time after time into other remnants—great empires, little kingdoms, minor robber chiefs rose, flourished and fell. War was the eternal order of things. There was one great border made out of a thousand small borders, all of them turbulent and troubled forever by raids, incursions, battles, sieges, rapine and loot. Above all the clamor, and most terrible and insistent, rose at not infrequent intervals the migrant thunder of the Tartar drums. Out of all this turmoil of incident grew epics, stories and legends that were old before the west was young. Great conquerors left the stories of their deeds. Heroes were immortalized by poets. Tribal boastings and robber deeds of daring-do, mixed with the dolorous tales of forlorn lovers fit for the zenana, became the stock in trade of bards and turbaned troubadors and the evening amusement of countless campfires and generations of firesides.

All of which brings us more immediately to the material at hand.

Northwest of India there is a great tract of mountainous and plateau country long occupied by a warlike and predominantly Mohammedan people. Such words as Afghanistan, Baluchistan, Kabul, and Samarkand bring it most familiarly and yet always mysteriously and glamourously to western minds. It is the very essence of the great Central Asian Borderland, *the* Border between Persia and India, a sort of buffer country between two different types of civilizations. Its tribesmen are mountaineers defending their own country fanatically and yet raiding habitually, especially southward and easterly. To the northwest in Persia grew up a highly polished literature centering about the Persian Court; to the south in India that literature introduced by Aryan conquerors underwent such changes in contact with Hindu letters as to render it a new and different thing. Polished and polite in its own way, it yet retained the impress of its classic origin. Between these two, and greatly affected by both of them, the mountaineers of the border countries, especially in Afghanistan, continued to cherish and to produce a type of literature that has long been recognized as typical of mountainous and frontier lands. To western and English-speaking peoples the nearest analogy in their own tradition is perhaps the legend and balladry of the Scotch Border. But the analogy is only true with a great difference. For the border, out of which come the poems here translated, is vastly huger in its physical aspects, infinitely more perplexed in its religious, racial, and political cleavages, and old as its mountains when Ossian was supposed to be celebrating a victory over the King of the World.

While both the polite and historical literatures of Persia and Mohammedan India have been extensively translated by and for western eyes, this is not nearly so true for the more remote and less known tongues and dialects of the great borderland, of which Afghanistan is typical. Achmed Abdullah may therefore be said in this book to have rendered a considerable service in making available in exact and yet highly readable form the poems in the Afghan, Persian, Turkoman, Tarantchi, Bokharan, Balochi, and Tartar idioms which he here presents, most of them for the first time in English. That, however, is merely by the way. To the great majority of readers the main interest will undoubtedly be in the racy vigor and unusual cast of the poems themselves.

For the vein which the translator has here tapped is obviously a peculiarly rich one. In it is combined very curiously the wrought gold of oriental character and the rough iron of universal human nature. Since, "Tis distance lends enchantment to the view," to western eyes at least many of the scenes and incidents of these poems must, despite the fact that they are stark realism, take on the pleasant glow of the romantic. Yet the romance here will be curiously blent with the fatalistic irony of the Mohammedan Asiatic, and shot through with an occasional sardonic twist that an occidental might be at some pains to charitably dissemble or even to disregard. Cruelty and obscenity, those two *bêtes noires* of English literature, lend a spice to oriental manuscripts that is here, although chiefly by inference, plainly at work. Without keeping this in mind much of the humor of these poems will be lost on the reader. There is inherent in many of them a racy native tinge which the translator has faithfully reproduced. In addition to this he has also embodied in the notes which accompany the poems all the information necessary to make clear both the immediate source and the particular allusions in each case. Hence the only legitimate object of the preface is to call the more general facts to mind.

In general then, it should be remembered that the poems here translated are not "book poetry," but verses fresh from the oral well-spring of literature — legends, stories, laments, boastings, and love songs — in short the very stuff of balladry, composed to be sung, chanted, or recited by tribal bards and other persons whom the spirit may move. The audience may be envisaged variously — sometimes a single individual kindly disposed toward the lyrical lucubrations of a friend, boastful or pathetic as the case may be, an idle group in a bazaar hopeful of a narrative with a kick, or more generally a tribal group gathered about the evening fires for an interlude of relaxation. Of such a tribal gathering in the "town-hall" or *hujra*, as it is called in Afghanistan, the translator has himself given us the very scene to the life in one of his superb stories.

"With the day's work done, the seeding well strewn, the long-haired, shaggy cattle lowing in the pens, the full-uddered goats leaping home from the upper pastures — there is music and rejoicing and laughter in the *hujra*, the communal hall of the tribe that faces the simple village mosque with the pride of stout walls and a great thatched roof.

It is an old Afghan peasant custom, this meeting on a spring evening, in the *hujra*. They would gather here, men and women — women of the North, free, unveiled, high-coloured, strong-bosomed — and smoke and drink tea and munch dried sunflower seeds and swap the news of the day. There would be, too, chiefly if a stranger, a traveling Bokharan trader or Persian caravanman, had passed through the valley, rumors of the far places; of tribal feud on the turbulent frontier; of a salty scandal amongst the Amir's grandees at the court of Kabul; of political intrigues in Moscow and Peking and Calcutta; of a British army column wiped out by the savage Waziris of the Indian Border, and envious comment: *"Hayah!* the grand, brave looting! And all to gorge the gullets of those lousy southerners!" — until finally, when the news had been told and re-told and spiced with good-natured, coarse jesting of the hills, some old man would clap his hands to enjoin silence . . . And then a great roaring of ancient ballads and a trilling of *misras*, songs improvised on the spur of the moment in which the singer glorifies his own or his tribe's prowess, or croons a melody of love . . . Thus the *hujra* to-night as always . . . Men and women. Old and young. Some squatted on their heels, pulling noisily at the jade or amber stems of gurgling water pipes. Others . . . stretched out on camel's-hair rugs or on soft beds of springy, scented spruce boughs, their backs to the large fir logs that crackled in the fireplaces since here, in the North, even May has a touch of frost.

At the very end of the room, facing them as an actor faces an audience . . . a man, six and a half foot of brawn and muscle and bone from his head to his ankles: seeming all the taller for an owl's gray wing that juts at a slant above his immense, shaggy fur cap, almost scraping the rafters: seeming all the broader for a snow-leopard's pelt rolled around his thick chest . . . His face is raised at a keen angle on the square, flagging chin; and above it the beaked nose with the flaring, nervous nostrils, throwing a purple shadow across high cheek-bones; the moustache brushed up aggressively until its points threaten the black eyes . . . then — a flash of even white teeth as, with pursed lips and the sweetest voice in all the world's hills, he sings an old Afghan ballad . . ." *

It is to such songs and to such singers that the poems in this book introduce us, songs snatched, as it were, hot from the lips

* *Steel and Jade* by Achmed Abdullah. N.Y. 1927.

11

of those who still sing them at the *hujra*. The rendering has been able, the translator is familiar with, is indeed, one of the people whose songs he here translates. In addition to that he is a versatile and distinguished writer in several occidental languages. Here he has caught up into English the feel and pull of his own idiom and successfully carried it over from the East to the West. The reader will be confronted, therefore, in these pages not with what is so often called, for lack of understanding, "the mysterious subtlety of the Orient," but with the brutal frankness and directness of it.

And, if he is a curious reader from a standpoint of style, he will also be able to note in passing that the usual ear-marks of border balladry are nearly all present. Here are to be found the choral refrain, the catchword or phrase, the stanza to be recited all in one breath, the apostrophe of the beloved or heroic name, a martial and even feudal code of honor. For this is not a mechanized or a democratic world that we enter upon. It is aristocratic, primal, and turbulent. Its denizens avow a contempt for the basely born and the foreigner; pride of race and place, and a fiery religious faith. Intolerance is theirs; their superstitions are prevalent and picturesque.

And through all of these poems run familiar allusions to legends, romances and historical occurrences that are as familiar to the people who employ them as are quotations from the Koran. It is these last in particular that the full notes of the translator serve to bring home vividly to the reader, thus rendering it superfluous for the prefacer to undertake, what is always most odious in any preface to a book of poems — a laborious explanation.

HERVEY ALLEN

Contents

Introduction

A GOOD many years ago — I was living in Paris at the time and had grown to be so ultra-French, ultra-French of a sort, that I wore monocle and white carnation and ran around with a gang of aristocratic young ruffians who called themselves *les camelots du roi* and assaulted everybody who believed in republican institutions or whose nose had the slightest Hebraic curve — a good many years ago, quite suddenly and quite unreasonably, I became conscious of a sharp sensation of homesickness. I became conscious, by the same token, of bitter-sweet imaginings about the Central Asia of my early youth. I remembered the towering mountains, an eternal, sardonic nose-thumbing against both British and Russian imperialistic kleptomania. I remembered the broad sweep of yellow, brittle summer across the steppes. I remembered the long, white, blighting winter months across these same steppes. I remembered the hard little hamlets tucked neatly into the fold of the bistre-brown foot-hills. I remembered the ancient towns wiped by the hand of time into blurred patterns . . . towns with cruel, rapacious hearts that regretted the days when the Tartar crescent trod the Nordic Cross under spurred heel; towns still redolent of the dead centuries when fur-capped Grand Khans sent arrogant edicts — edicts implicitly obeyed — to Christian monarchs, when the flat-faced, copper-skinned riders of the Golden Horde whipped their shaggy ponies to the loot of a shuddering western world, while other Moslem warriors poured through the Afghan passes to the conquest of Hindustan.

So I went home. To Afghanistan. Also to the cousinly lands of Russian Turkestan and Chinese Turkestan . . . High Tartary — I have always liked the old appellation.

And on the way I collected, not things, not bits of cracked Persian porcelain in dove-blue or frayed scraps of silken Bokharan rugs, but memories — nostalgic pictures — rapidly etched impressions of mosques swelling like the tolling of bells beneath a steel-gray, vaulted sky; of dwarfish idols, reminiscent of the days before Islam swamped the Buddha's gentler creed, glowing from their iron-barred wayside shrines in the light of seven crimson, panegyrical candles; of the massive projections of square, granite-clouted bastions chanting the epic of vanished dynasties; of palaces of Khan and Amir and Sultan tearing the heavens with clawlike copings and turrets; of purple nights on the steppes and the green stars sneering down with a sort of cosmic insouciance; of ruddy harvests climbing up to the hyacinth of the lower hills; of the high, far, lonely mountains where — as we say in the Afghan tongue — the free men, the strong men, the hearty men live on the wind and the pines and the gray rock's lichen.

Impressions of all that Central Asian scattering and queer, sudden converging of line and color, wholly without set design and wholly without evident logic or purpose — therefore the opposite of Europe where life, civilization, culture, call it what you will, is rather like a problem in abstract dynamics — and yet throbbing with the grand rhythm of a distinct racial elegy.

There were, too, other impressions, more human and more poignant, to be collected and stored away against the coming of homesick dreams . . . perhaps, since writing is my craft, against the coming of novels and plays and short stories yet to be plotted. Impressions of crowds and individuals, Asiatics and Europeans, bubbling in the same cauldron of cheating and lies — international trade and international politics, in other words. Impressions of the crash of race against race, faith against faith, civilization against civilization. Impressions of the trade-marks of Russia's jostling progress from the north — a railway depot, a cabaret, a German cocotte, a printing-press, and a sergeant of infantry getting dismally drunk upon vodka — jutting sharply into the veiled, fanatical focus of Tartar life and prejudices; impressions of Great Britain's gliding progress from the south — a snobbish junior judge, a church, a bundle of bald commercial statistics, an Anglo-Saxon spinster writing silly books, and a sergeant of cavalry getting rowdyishly drunk upon whiskey — jutting sharply into the violent, fanatical focus of Afghan life and prejudices.

Dozens of impressions. Still my homesickness persisted. So, finally, I cut clear away from the last Russian and British outpost and, for nearly a year, I traveled "native" — native in dress, speech, food, drink, mode of thought — through Afghanistan, through Russian and Chinese Turkestan, and into Outer Mongolia.

And, as I traveled, I listened.

I listened to the ancient folk tales, the ancient folk songs and ballads few of which have ever been written down; and there, at last, I found what I was after.

Then I remembered other folk songs and ballads from my childhood days; and, when I had returned to Europe, I wrote to my youngest sister, residing in India, who has her old Tartar-Afghan nurse still living with her. I asked her to have the old nurse dictate to her whatever folk songs she could recall.

So, ultimately, I had quite a collection of crude, homespun poems. I translated and annotated them and made what I consider a representative selection.

They are, to me at least, more than mere folk poetry. They are the very spirit, the very marrow of our Central Asian life.

But — let them speak for themselves. . . .

ACHMED ABDULLAH

Lute and Scimitar

The Sword — Is It Sharpened for the Blow . . .

◆

This poem, of the early seventeenth century, is attributed by some to Khushal Khan, a chief of the warlike Khatak tribe of Afghans who lived near the Kaibar Pass during the days when Shah Jehan and Aurangzeb were the Mogul emperors at Delhi. Others claim it to be a traditional poem of the licentious Rushumya sect of Moslem Sufis, founded at Kabul, during the reign of the Mogul emperor Akbar, by one Bayazid Ansari who was called by his enemies the '*Peri Tarik*' or 'Apostle of Darkness' in derision of the title of '*Peri Rushun*' or 'Apostle of Light' which he had assumed. The Rushumya sect which, influenced by Hinduism, believed in the transmigration of souls, was excommunicated by successive Sheykhs-ul-Islam. (*From the southern Afghan*)

◆

The sword — is it sharpened for the blow?
  Is it?
   Or is it not?
Your hair — is it curled for the touch of my
  hands?
  Is it?
  Or is it not?
Then why say to me: 'Look not at my fair
  face!'
My eyes — did Allah create them for seeing?
  Did He?
  Or did He not?

Let the priests fast and babble their prayers.
Let topers raise their goblets filled with wine.
Every man has been created to live his own life.
  Is it so?
  Or is it not?

You said: 'My mouth's touch is a healing drug.'
Let me drink it — to heal my heart's wound.
    Will it?
    Or will it not?

Your tongue sucks the marrow from my soul.
       My soul is yours.
    Is it?
    Or is it not?
Compared to you, like weeds are the rose and
       tulip.
    Are they?
    Or are they not?

Here is sweet wine. Here golden lute and flute.
Here is my mistress. Here my desire — and
       her promise.
Here is the red, red garden.
    Will I hasten there?
    Or will I not?

In the Courtyard of Afzal Khan...

◆

I heard this poem in the Hazaureh Mountains, southwest of Kabul, where to this day live certain isolated settlements of Balochis. They are on the best of terms with the surrounding Afghan tribesmen, but speak their own language. The poem dates back to the early nineteenth century. At that time the Afghan dynasty founded by Ahmad Shah had degenerated, and Peshawar had fallen into the hands of four of the famous twelve Barukzai brothers, the Sirdars Yar Mohammed, Sultan Mohammed, Pir Mohammed, and Sayyid Mohammed. There was a great deal of confusion and war throughout Afghanistan and the border, Afghan fighting brother Afghan, Balochi irregulars joining in, and occasionally all combining to fight the growing menace of the Sikh nation under the great Ranjit Singh. This poem is attributed to Turkan Khatoom, the Afghan wife of Afzal Khan, a Balochi freebooter and captain in the army of the youngest of the Barukzai brothers who afterwards made himself Amir of Afghanistan. It appears that during a raid into India Afzal Khan kidnapped three women of the Sikhs whom he made his concubines; and Turkan Khatoom ridicules her new rivals' pretensions in the following intensely typical lines. (*From the Balochi*)

◆

*I*n the courtyard of Afzal Khan the little
    tree parrots
  Gaily flutter about.
  Hear how the silly little parrots twitter and
    chirp!
See how they preen their gaudy Indian feathers!

  They fly from tree to tree.
  Wherever they fly, they drop their dung.
  Dirty, garish little Indian parrots!

23

In the very courtyard of Hydar Khan's grand-
    son
The little tree parrots flutter and flutter.
Yet should I, the tough old Afghan hawk, fear
    them?

Tomorrow Afzal Khan will have grown tired of
    them.
Tomorrow he will wring their silly little necks.
But I am Turkan Khatoom.
Seven sons have I borne my lord!

Ali Bek, the Yoozbashee . . .

◆

This is a poem of the Bokharan Uzbeks. The Uzbeks invaded Central Asia not long after the death of Tamerlane who, in his famous Autobiography, refers to them as "heathen Mongols from the Jaxartes river." Since then they have been converted to Islam and have become the ruling, military clan in the Central Asian Khanates of Bokhara, Khiva, and Khokand. Though inferior numerically, nor as clever commercially as the Central Asian Aryans — the Persians, Sarts, Tajiks and Badakshanis — they have influenced the country to such a degree that the Aryan inhabitants, given the slightest excuse, try to claim the honored distinction of being Uzbeks. They are a roystering, rowdy-ish breed; yet — strange to say — most of their poetry has a distinctly Sunday-schoolish flavor. A *"Yoozbashee,"* referred to in this poem, means an "officer of a hundred," an army captain, exactly like a Roman centurion. (*From the Bokharan*)

◆

Ali Bek, the Yoozbashee, has three wives.
They are comely and virtuous. But he is
*   never home.*
All day he drinks wine like a Christian, smokes
*   opium,*
And kisses the full-lipped daughters of the
*   damnèd Jews.*

Yakoob and Daud are his two young sons.
Nobody watches the stepping of their feet.
At home they hear no sound at all
Except their mothers, crying their eyes out.

So Yakoob and Daud leave the house.
They, too, drink wine like Christians, smoke
*   opium,*
And kiss the full-lipped daughters of the damnèd
*   Jews.*
They, too, trample on every law of the sainted
*   Koran.*

25

Ali Bek, the Yoozbashee, hears the gossip of it.
So, with blows and curses, he admonishes his
    sons
Because they had put their feet upon a path of
    life
Fully as wicked and ungodly as his own.

An old man witnesses the scene, and says to him:
'Consider, O Yoozbashee, that when the master
    beats the drum,
Has he then the right to blame his children
Because they dance to the tune he plays?'

Lullaby to My Little Son ...

◆

This is a cradle-song of the Turkolani Afghans who live in the vicinity of the Kaibar Pass near Peshawar on both sides of the border. The Mohammedzyes, mentioned in the poem, are their neighbors, both tribes being branches of the great Eusufzye clan which, until the fourteenth century, lived on the outskirts of the *"Dushtee Lut"* or Great Salt Desert, now part of the Indian Empire and inhabited by Balochis. After leaving the *"Dushtee Lut"* they settled farther north, in the high mountains about Kabul where, for several generations, they were in high favor with the descendants of Tamerlane. But, notorious even in Afghanistan for their rowdy manners and savage independence, Mirza Ulugh Bek, of the house of Tamerlane, was finally forced to drive all the Eusufzyes south again to their present habitations where they have been settled for over three hundred years now. This cradle-song is similar to many that are sung in the hills throughout Afghanistan, Balochistan, and parts of Turkestan with slight variations often impromptu, added by the mothers on the spur of the moment. (*From the border Afghan*)

◆

Lullaby to my little son!
    Lullaby to Murad Hydar, my little
        son!
May God and the Prophet bless him!
May he be blessed by the Four Com-
    panions,
The Twelve Apostles, the Fourteen Holy
    Innocents,
And the Forty-Seven Excellent Saints!

May Murad Hydar, my little son, grow into
    strong, lusty manhood,
And bind about his forehead a large white
    turban,
Throw a great red cloak about his shoulders,
And take to hand and elbow the five weapons of
    the Afghans:
Buckler, rifle, dagger, knotted whip of rawhide,
And a shining sword out of Persia.

May he mount his slender mare and ride down
    the hills,
And go at night to the villages of the dirty-
    robed Mohammedzyes,
And entice away with sweet speech the flower of
    their maidens,
A chief's daughter, red and white,
With smooth face, all hair shaved off her body,
Small, pointed breasts, each large enough to
    fill a hand,
And with black tresses like female cobras.
May he wing along the mountains like a hawk,
And swoop, unerring, upon the little partridge
    of the Mohammedzyes.

And she will say to my little son:
    'When the sun dies red and gold behind the
        hills,
    When the moon is stabbed on the outer horns
        of the world,
    Then you must tie your slender mare
    Behind the tamarisk, and wait.
    You must wait until my father goes out to
        the pasture,
    To drive home our small cattle,
    And until my dreadful old grandmother
    Stills her leaky tongue and goes to sleep.
    Then I shall meet you in the place you know,
    And lie down beside you,
    My lips to yours, my thighs to yours,
    And we will rest in joy until the morning
        star shines green.
    And then you must quickly go away,
    Lest my father awake, or my dreadful old
        grandmother.'

May Murad Hydar, my little son, grow into
    stout, lusty manhood,

And redden his hands with his enemies' blood,
As the falcon of the hills dyes red his talons.
For there will be bitter strife with the Moham-
    medzyes,
The wearers of dirty turbans,
And the chief of the Turkolanis will send word
To Murad Hydar, my little son, to lead the
    vanguard.
And my little son will gather his troop of horse-
    men,
And will crush the hounds of the Mohammedz yes
As a booted foot crushes the head of a cobra.

Lullaby to my little son!
May the Single, Eternal God bless him!

Come Tonight, O Beloved ...

◆

This love ballad is by Nur Shah Ali, an Afghan poet of the early nineteenth century. Love and war are the only two themes of which the hill people sing. In both love and war poems, form as well as substance has become highly conventionalized, almost monotonous to the western ear. But in the original Afghan the poems contain a number of metaphors and plays on words which lose sense and significance in an English translation. (*From the northern Afghan*)

◆

Come tonight, O beloved. Come and
        hurry.
        I shall meet you at the corner of the road
When you and the other young girls return from
        the well.

'Come tonight, O strong man. Come and
        hurry.
I am your little nightingale.
When the young girls heard you calling me,
They left me alone at the corner of the road.
Come tonight. Come and hurry.
I shall give you the flower of my red mouth
        and the forest of my black locks.'

Come tonight.
Come and hurry, O my beloved.

* * *

'I have loosened my black locks. I am naked.
Look at me, O strong man.
Take my hand, without fear.
For my father has left the house.
Come and sit by my side on the red bed.
I am waiting.'

Come tonight.
Come and hurry, O my beloved.

'Sit by my side on the red bed.
I give you my lips that are scarlet with the
    scarlet of my heart.
Your hairy hands are crushing my white
    breasts, O strong man.
My beauty is a garden.
You are the hawk in the beauty of my
    garden.'

Come tonight.
Come and hurry, O my beloved.

* * *

'My beauty is a garden.
Dark are the flowers in the secret paths of my
    garden.'

I cannot reach the secret flowers in the beauty
    of your garden.
They are surrounded by the thick jungle of your
    black hair.
Three or four little beauty spots are on your
    small chin.
Nur Shah Ali desires your soft and delicate
    lips.

Come tonight.
Come and hurry, O my beloved.

Listen to My Words,
O Moslems...

◆

This poem, of the late eighteenth century, comes from Yaghistan. It is a *ghazal*, a form of poetry not native to Afghanistan, but borrowed from Persia, which is used only by the *sha'ir*, the polite poet of city and court who knows his Hafiz and Sa'di, and never by the rough, illiterate *dum* or village bard, the real poet of the hills who improvises his verses at night in the *huira* or communal council hall, accompanying himself on the *rebab* or Afghan guitar. This *ghazal* is interestingly reminiscent of Villon's: "*Où sont les neiges d'antan?*," and also of the famous Persian poem which begins:

> "*Kuja an Feridoon, Zohak o Djem,*
> *Shahan Arab, o Khosrouan Agem?* —
> Where are Feridoon, Sohak and Jemshid,
> The kings of Arabia and Persia's emperors?"

(*From the northern Afghan*)

◆

L isten to my words, O Moslems!
   All the world's pride returns to dust.
   So take with you to your graves a few
            truths,
That in the hereafter you may have no regrets.

For where is Abraham, the friend of God?
And Ismail, His sacrifice?
Where is the Prophet Mohammed who wore the
            halo of the Blest,
Though he never climbed the peak of Mount
            Sinai?
And Jesus, the sweet Saint? Where is he?
Hai! Hai!
The wind has blown their dust away!

Where is the emperor Akbar? And where went
            Mohammed Shah?
Tell me: where is Aurangzeb, the mighty
            Mogul?

And where all the strong men of the Fatimide
     dynasty?
Hai! Hai!
Sighing they went to their graves!

Where is Gengiz Khan, the conqueror of black
     China?
And Kublai Khan, the thunderer?
Where is Nadir Shah, the Turkoman?
Where is Uzbek Khan of the Golden Horde who
     enslaved the Russians?
Hai! Hai!
Today their riches are but brittle vanity.
For the end is the end. The end is nothing.

You have forgotten the Lord God, O Moslems!
But the tomb will be your fatherland. All
     earthly pomp matters not.
So turn your thoughts to Allah and curse Satan
     the Stoned!
The end is the end. The end is nothing.
For where is Ghirei, the Khan of the Crimea?
Hai! Hai!
The wind has dried up his blood!

Death will come, riding his black camel.
On that day none will help you except the
     Lord God.
The end is the end. The end is nothing.
Hai! Hai!
The wind will blow your pride away!

Tell me: Where are Sultans and Khans and
     Amirs?
Where went Alexander of Macedon?
Osman of Samarkand — where went he?
And Wang Khan, the ape-faced Manchu?
Hai! Hai!
The wind has blown their swords away!

*Tomorrow, your foreheads black with sin, you
will go to the grave.*
*Tomorrow the end will be the end. The end
is nothing.*
Today is the hour of religion, O Moslems.
*Do good deeds! Pray! Oppress not the
orphans!*
*Tomorrow — hai! hai! — the wind will blow
your bones away!*
*So bow before the Lord God, King of the Day of
Judgment!*
His glory shines across the seven worlds!
Only by His grace splendor is in Islam!

I Said: If I Come To You...

◆

There exist several versions of the following poem which dates back to the seventeenth century. One, like most songs of that period, has been attributed to Khushal Khan, chief of the Khatak tribe of Afghans. A second version, and an earlier one, is credited to Mir Gwaharam, chief of the Lashari tribe of Balochis, and written by him to the lady Gohar who, later on, took refuge with Mir Chakur, the chief of the Rind tribe of Balochis . . . which, incidentally, caused the thirty years' war between the two tribes of which the hillmen still sing numerous ballads. The third version — which I am using — is recited and sung to this day by the small colony of Turkoman-speaking Kalmicks settled in Kabul. (*From the Turkoman*)

◆

"*I said:*
If I come to you, will your lips kiss mine?"
    She said:
"*Have you a thousand lips that you should
    ask me?*"

    I said:
"*Your raven locks are like black cobras.*"
    She said:
"*Fool — would you trust a hooded cobra's
    sting?*"

    I said:
"*How then shall I conquer your love?*"
    She said:
"*Can you cut off a head without a sword?*"

    I said:
"*Like a blind pilgrim, I wander aimlessly.*"
    She said:
"*If you are a wise pilgrim, why disgrace your-
    self?*"
    I said:
"*Let us be happy together, if only for a
    moment.*"

She said:

"What happened to the women whom you used to love?"

I said:

"You are proud. Consider that Allah does not like the proud."

She said:

"Why yell so loudly? What matters my pride to you?"

I said:

"I am the lover of your small, golden face."

She said:

"Allah! Do not force your foul love on me!"

I said:

"If I die on your threshold, yours will be the blame."

She said:

"Go and die. Then my dogs will no longer bark."

I said:

"You cannot understand the love which I bear you."

She said:

"And what does a Kalmick know of love?"

I Grant That Famed . . .

◆

This poem, of the early seventeenth century, by Khushal Khan, the chief of the Khatak tribe of Afghans, has always amused me greatly, not because of what it says, but because of what it does not say. I cannot help but feel that the Khan, vicariously, in thus praising the Afghan women, is taking a "dirty dig" at the women of other lands. For, in his younger years, Khushal Khan was a great lover. Later on he reformed. A partial result of his moral reform seems to be contained in the following lines. (*From the southern Afghan*)

◆

I grant that famed for their beauty are the
    women of China,
  Of Kashmir, Bokhara, and the land of
    High Tartary.
Yet mine own eyes have beheld the maidens
    of the Afghans.
Why then, hereafter, should I look on other
    women?

Pure is their race. Of the lineage of Jacob
    are they.
They need neither musk nor attar of red roses.
For is there a sweeter scent than the scent of
    their piety,
Praying five times each day to Allah, the King,
    the One?

They need neither bracelets nor nose-rings nor
    necklaces,
Since, more precious than jewels, are their black
    tresses.
They need no embroidered shawls, no robes of
    scarlet muslin,
Preferring the exquisite chastity of simple
    white face veils.

Sweeter are their hidden charms than those
    flaunted by shameless foreign women.

37

For the maidens of Afghanistan are virtuous.
They spend their time in the seclusion of their
    homes,
And go not about, like others I know, with their
    bodies half-naked.

They are so modest that they never drop their
    face veils
And raise bold eyes to passersby in the bazaars.
They do not curse their men; nor nag them;
Nor clench fists in red anger.

And I, Khushal Khan of the Khatak,
Have spoken but little of what is much.
Silent I shall be on this matter, though it is
    boundless.

Last Night I Went for a Stroll . . .

◆

The following ballad was written in the sixties of the last century by Mohammedji, the Afghan poet, and is one of the very few Afghan poems of which there exists an English translation. Mr. E. Powys Mathers made such a translation; did it with consummate artistry; nor can I hope to rival or better his. My only intention is to interest students of Oriental literature by giving a translation which will record the original text word for word. Mohammedji, incidentally, was not a very savory character. A native of Pakli, he wandered all through the hills and, fond of drunken brawls and in the habit of making love to other men's wives, he knew the inside of many an Afghan and Indian prison. (*From the northern Afghan*)

◆

L ast night I went for a stroll
In the bazaar of black locks.
Like a bee I sipped honey
In the bazaar of black locks.

Last night I strolled leisurely
Through the garden of black locks.
Like a bee I sucked the voluptuous sugar
Of my mistress' pomegranate breasts.
My biting teeth tasted the pure gold
Of her little ears and of her throat,
And I inhaled the cloying scent of the garland
about my queen's neck,
The garland of black locks.

Last night I went for a stroll
In the bazaar of black locks.
Like a bee I sipped honey
In the bazaar of black locks.

* * *

'You inhaled the scent of my body, O my
friend,

39

And it intoxicated you like opium.
You fell asleep as did Bahram on Sarasya's
　　bed.
But there is one who hates you for having
　　stolen my kisses.
He, the guardian of black locks, has given
　　oath
To cut off your head with his snake-like
　　sword.'

Last night I went for a stroll
In the bazaar of black locks.
Like a bee I sipped honey
In the bazaar of black locks.

* * *

'Does he indeed hate me, best beloved?
Allah will protect me — have no fear!
Give me, for my defence, a club made of your
　　long black locks.
And give me your small white face.
I hunger for its kisses like a little parrot.
Permit me to lose my way in the jungle of
　　black locks.'

Last night I went for a stroll
In the bazaar of black locks.
Like a bee I sipped honey
In the bazaar of black locks.

* * *

'I will grant you entrance, O my friend,
Into the scented, moist garden of my white
　　body.
But afterwards you will treat me with con-
　　tempt and leave me.
And yet, when I show the white beauty of
　　my body,

The lamp's yellow light is like darkness.
O Allah, let me cover my nakedness
With the cloak of my black locks!'

Last night I went for a stroll
In the bazaar of black locks.
Like a bee I sipped honey
In the bazaar of black locks.

*   *   *

'Allah gave to you exquisite beauty.
Cast me a look, O rejoicer. I am your little
    slave.
Early yesterday morning I sent the old
    woman with a message for you.
A snake has stung my heart,
The snake of your black locks.'

Last night I went for a stroll
In the bazaar of black locks.
Like a bee I sipped honey
In the bazaar of black locks.

*   *   *

'I shall charm the snake with the breath of my
    lips, O my friend.
But my honor is torn to pieces.
Come. Take me away from Pakli.
My husband is a beast. He disgusts me.
I give you complete power over my black
    locks.'

Last night I went for a stroll
In the bazaar of black locks.
Like a bee I sipped honey
In the bazaar of black locks.

* * *

I, Mohammedji the Afghan, have power over
  all the poets of Pakli.
By force I take tax from the Amirs of Delhi.
I rule my kingdom with a sword and sceptre of
  black locks.

Last night I went for a stroll
In the bazaar of black locks.
Like a bee I sipped honey
In the bazaar of black locks.

There, In Night's Great Purple Box ...

◆

This is a poem of the Tarantchis who live about Kuldja in Eastern Turkestan, on the Russian-Chinese border. Their language, except for certain influences due to the colonies of Kalmicks, Chinese and Manchus who live amongst them, is a very pure Turki, in fact purer than the modern Turkish spoken in Constantinople. They are mostly peasants, their very name meaning "millet-sowers," from *"taran — millet."* They are Moslems and claim descent from the ancient Uigur tribe of Tartar-Mongols, once famed for their learning. (*From the Tarantchi*)

◆

There, in night's great purple box,
I hid my seven jewels:
My women, my children, my horses,
My honor, my sword, my faith, and my race.
Solitude watches carefully,
So that none may steal them.

Three stout locks has the box which hides my
*   jewels.*
Let him who has jewels lock them with three
*   locks:*
With silence, and mockery, and laughter!

In Spite of All My Misfortunes . . .

◆

This poem was written by Khushal Khan, chief of the Khatak tribe of Afghans, in the late seventeenth century during the period of his imprisonment by Aurungzeb, the Mogul Emperor of India. It is his shortest poem; but I have an idea that it is most typical, not only of himself, but of all the Afghan nation. (*From the southern Afghan*)

◆

In spite of all my misfortunes, I am still grateful to Allah for two things: The first is that I am an Afghan; the second that I am Khushal Khan, the Khatak.

Mohammed Jan, the Warrior...

◆

In the year 1879 Sir Louis Napoleon Cavagnari, British envoy at Kabul, was murdered by order of the Amir of the Afghans. England, thereupon, invaded Afghanistan, the army being commanded by Lord Roberts who, after initial successes, was besieged in his camp at Sherpur, whence he only escaped by the skin of his teeth. To this day the hills ring with martial ballads, reminiscent of this war. The following has all the earmarks of a nursery song with its refrain:

> "*Biya basha am angar bakhoor* —
> Come, little son, let us eat grapes."

But it carries a double meaning. For it also refers to Lord Roberts' critical situation at Sherpur, and is a sardonic comment on the careless nurse, Lord Roberts, asking his little son, the British-Indian army, to eat grapes — anglicé: not to worry — in spite of the terrible danger. To understand better certain allusions in the poem, let me explain that Daud Shah was bribed by the English; so was Vali Mohammed Khan; that Abderrahman Khan, afterward Amir of the Afghans, was then an exile in Russia under the Tsar's protection; that the son of Mohammed Shareef Khan, brother of Shir Ali, former Amir of the Afghans, was playing both ends against the middle, being bribed today by Russia, tomorrow by England, and even tried to sell out to the Emperor of China. The "double rupees" referred to are the British-Indian rupees which are worth twice the Afghan rupees. The reference to Teheran means that the Afghans might try to draw Persia into the war by ceding to her Herat which was formerly a Persian town. Mohammed Jan, finally, was the great national Afghan leader and hero, a man who rose from the ranks. (*From the border Afghan*)

◆

Mohammed Jan, the warrior, is our hero —
Come, little son, let us eat grapes.

He commands our soldiers on the field of battle —
Come, little son, let us eat grapes.

Daud Shah is a bastard —
Come, little son, let us eat grapes.

Vali Mohammed Khan is a demon —
Come, little son, let us eat grapes.

Yakub Khan is a loyal gentleman —
Come, little son, let us eat grapes.

Musa Khan is the Amir of the Afghans —
Come, little son, let us eat grapes.

Abderrahman Khan is the child of the Tsar —
Come, little son, let us eat grapes.

Asmatullah Khan is at Kashman —
Come, little son, let us eat grapes.

Mohammed Shareef Khan is in prison —
Come, little son, let us eat grapes.

His son is a vile stench in our nostrils —
Come, little son, let us eat grapes.

Kabul has become Hindu —
Come, little son, let us eat grapes.

Our women are widowed —
Come, little son, let us eat grapes.

But there is yet a great battle to be fought —
Come, little son, let us eat grapes.

The decision will rest with Iran —
Come, little son, let us eat grapes.

All the plains are blood-red with flowers —
Come, little son, let us eat grapes.

The roses are red with the martyrs' blood —
Come, little son, let us eat grapes.

On all sides fly double rupees —
Come, little son, let us eat grapes.

Herat belongs to Teheran —
Come, little son, let us eat grapes.

Ayoob Khan is at his wits' end —
Come, little son, let us eat grapes.

Red, Red Were the Flowers...

◆

The following ballad, written by Ali Jan, refers, like the preceding, to the war of 1886 when the British under Lord Roberts invaded Afghanistan and, through their victory at Sar Asya, had Kabul at their mercy. The Mullah Khalil referred to in the poem was a Moslem priest and a favorite of the Sahib of Sowatt, who preached Holy War throughout the hills. Malik Shafi, cousin and bitterest enemy of Abderrahman Khan, afterwards Amir of the Afghans but then still an exile in Russia, had been bribed by the British and lived under their protection at Peshawar. (*From the northern Afghan*)

◆

*Red, red were the flowers of martyrdom that
          bloomed on the hills of Sar Asya.
     Many martyrs went to war.
They were cut to pieces by the shining swords.*

*Look at Mullah Khalil, the man of God!
What force he has, what grand eloquence!
From village to village he went, preaching
          Holy War,
And all the young warriors followed him, with
          their snake-like swords.*

*Kashkot came and Goriaki; Surk and Masar;
          and the Budyalvals and Dari-
          Noris.
But as soon as they heard the thunder of the
          British guns,
Those pigs ran away.*

*Mullah Khalil spoke:
"I could not give battle. God's mercy on
          me!
I preached the word of the Prophet!
But the hillmen ran away, with their faces where
          their buttocks should have been!"*

There came a sudden noise.
An English squadron galloped toward Sar
    Asya.
And Karun Khan cried:
"Here rides the Commissioner of Severed
    Heads in storm and pomp!
Fly, men, for these people have come to slit
    our throats!"
And, led by that bastard Karun Khan,
The young men ran away toward the
    river.

Punish them, O All-Merciful Lord God!
    Destroy them utterly!
They are cowards and traitors!
There is no worth in them.
They ran away, and there came to Kabul black
    clouds and crimson battalions;
    English troops came in great numbers.
The banners of the unbelievers have been un-
    furled because those pigs,
Those fathers of pigs have run away.

God's mercy on the red flowers of martyr-
    dom of Kalai Malak!
They gave battle with the shining, twisting
    swords!
In the hereafter they will be the sweet-voiced
    nightingales in the heavenly
    garden!

But a thousand curses on Malik Shafi!
    He eats dung!
    He drinks camels' offal!
He took foreign gold and caused those pigs of
    hillmen to laugh in their throats.

But the sisters of Agha Jan, the martyr
weep.
They pray to Allah to send back to them their
martyred flower with the hand-
some face.
They desire to see again his green turban, his
shining sword, his red cloak, his
black eyes.

O Ali Jan!
Their deep grief is a heavy weight upon
your heart!

Misras...

◆

The *misras* are short poems of the border Afghans, similar to the *stornelli* of the Italians, the *dastanaghs* of the Balochis and the *dorhas* of the Punjaubis, and are sung to the accompaniment of a flute. A *misra* is supposed to be sung in one breath, the singer winding up, when his breath gives out, in a piercing sound, half yell and half gasp, fully two octaves higher than the song itself. It is a peculiarity that most of the *misras* deal with the singer's love for a married woman. The majority — since morals are different East and West — cannot be translated. The following, which I heard among the Afridis, are the mildest I know, and even then I had to edit them *à l'usage du dauphin*. (*From the border Afghan*)

◆

I

Blows the wind — slow, slow!
Sings the rain — cold, cold!
Waits the bed — warm, warm!
Beats my heart — strong, strong!
Gleam thy breasts — white, white!
Wind — rain — bed — heart — breasts!
Why wait, O wife of the red-bearded man?

II

Tie your husband with a rope, Bimbar, and
come to your lover!
Tie the rope to a tree, Bimbar, and come to
your lover!
Throw the tree in a river, Bimbar, and come to
your lover!

III

Give me your lips, girl of the Afridis;
My lips are hotter than your husband's.
Give me your arms, girl of the Afridis;
My arms are stronger than your husband's.

Give me your body, girl of the Afridis;
    My body is broader than your husband's.
Give me your love, girl of the Afridis;
    My love is sweeter than your husband's.

IV

Breathless with desire — I am on your track,
    girl.
With a rifle I stole from the English — I am
    on your track, girl.
Your husband is a camel — I am on your track,
    girl.
Tomorrow I shall kill him — I am on your
    track, girl.
Then the carrion-kites will fly low — I am on
    your track, girl.

Thee Do I Ask for Help...

◆

This poem, too, is by Khushal Khan, chief of the Khatak tribe. It is his confession of faith. Written at a time when esoteric Sufiism was rampant in Persia and when Omar Khayyam and similar third-rate poetasters were the fashion from Teheran to Kabul, while the Moslems of India were influenced and tainted by Hindu heathendom, it is purely and refreshingly Islamic and shows a sturdiness which is typically Afghan. With the change of a word here and there, it might have been written by a poetically inclined Scots clergyman of the "Free Kirk." (*From the southern Afghan*)

◆

Thee do I ask for help, O God, the One,
*   the Indivisible.*
Only beneath Thy shadow can I succeed.
I crouch on Thy threshold, Thy slave.   Thee
*   do I praise.*
Thee shall I praise while breath is in my body.

Thy mercies are without number, like the sands
*   of the desert.*
And who can count the sands?
Thou art beyond age and time.   Thou wast.
*   Thou remainest.*
Eternal art Thou, the One.

Thou alone, with help from none,
Hast created the earth, the seven heavens,
The two worlds, all humans and all animals.
Thy will, O God, created everything.
Yet none created Thee!

White or black, we are all but symbols of Thy
*   unity.*
All Thy works are wondrous, fashioned in
*   goodness,*

53

While the work of men's hands may be good or bad.
But Thou dost not close the door of mercy to the sinner.

Thus my confession of faith. Does my life agree with it?
No! My life stammers, though my words do not.
I do not deserve Thy Mercy.
Then help me to deserve it, O God, Eternal and One!

Lonely and Unadorned...

◆

This is a *"meit tauriki,"* similar to an epitaph, of the Karachuka Turkomans, a clan of the Yomud Turkomans who roam the Central Asian steppes near the Caspian. The Turkoman graves consist of underground chambers where the body is placed without covering, together with the earthen jug used in washing it. A small lamp is placed at the foot of the grave, as well as some article belonging to the deceased, usually a cradle in case of a child, but all these articles, given the Turkomans' harsh life, are simple and crude. The place where the head rests is marked by a stone called *"m'chachad"* which, curiously, is not a Turkoman but an Arab word. There is no verdure about the graves, no flowers, nothing to make them attractive. They are typical, in their stark, gray loneliness, of the steppes and the tribes of the steppes. (*From the Turkoman*)

◆

Lonely and unadorned is the last bed of the
     desert rider,
     When death seizes his throat as the
     eclipse seizes the moon,
When Fate gathers the thousand arrows be-
     neath her arm-pits.

There are here no gold-hilted Bokharan
     scimitars,
No crimson, jingling trappings of Turkish Beks,
No brocaded cloaks nor great belts of Volga
     leather.
     For naked I came from the bosom of God.
     Naked I return.

You, O pilgrim, when you ride past my grave,
     stop.
     Pass not without a thought for me.
Remember that only yesterday I was even as
     you.
Remember that tomorrow you will be even as I.

My Grief Has Ended...

◆

The following poem is by Khushal Khan, chief of the Khatak tribe of the Afghan nation, and dates from the late seventeenth century. The Afghans consider it one of the most charming love poems in their language. (*From the southern Afghan*)

◆

My grief has ended.
Comes now the season of joy.
For the flowers of Spring are jeweling my
green garden.
Let us make ready to walk through its paths.
Go! Tell the nightingale that Spring is here.

And tell the minstrel to come with his lute.
Let him sing us a ballad of the flowers of
Spring.
Do not listen to the parrot whispering to the
rose
That Autumn will soon be here.

With Spring my love returned to me,
And again I behold the moon of my delight.
Let others have their various festivals.
My only festival is when, in Spring,
I see my mistress' narrow feet
Step through the garden like lisping twin
flowers.

Then Khushal Khan puts on his brightest robes,
And he enters the bazaar of his mistress' soft
arms.

Timoor Khan, the Waziri...

◆

This poem, of the early sixteenth century, has come down in several versions. There is a Balochi version dating from the thirty years' war between the two tribes of Balochis, the Rinds and the Lasharis; other versions are sung in both Afghan and Persian Seistan; while the one which I am using is heard among the Afghan Waziris who live north of the western base of the Tukhti Suleyman. They drone rather than sing their poems, winding up the recitation with a sort of Pyrrhic war dance, leaping over crossed swords and flourishing their *cheray* daggers which look exactly like butcher's cleavers. The song refers to a Khan who, once rich and generous, lost all his possessions through gambling with the "colored knuckle-bones," was forced to flee his tribe and become an ostler for a widow of the Sharaunis, the tribe to the south of the Waziris. The humor of this poem is gloriously unconscious. The Waziris take it with utter seriousness. I have seen them — huge, broad-shouldered, bearded men — shed tears at Timoor Khan's fate .... (*From the border Afghan*)

◆

Timoor Khan, the Waziri, sings.
The sweet-voiced ancient sings.
On the subject of himself and
the colored knuckle-bones
He says a few words.

Once I drew my cheray from a green belt
studded with jewels.
And across my shoulders I threw a cloak of
crimson velvet,
Lined with fur and tied with scented leather
of Herat.
My followers were many.
Between the shadows of the shafts of their
threatening lances
Was no room to put a foot.

My fifty stallions were slender.
Many were the women whom I caused to wear
dark-blue in mourning

57

For their lovers whom I killed,
When my snake-like blade bit the heads from
their shoulders.

Now the toss of the colored knuckle-bones has
brought me low.
I have fled my round stone tower-house, my rich
encampment,
And the brilliant assemblies of my clan.
Now a pig-faced widow of the Sharaunes calls
me 'little uncle.'
She has put a sickle in my hands and bid me cut
the grass
For her seven spavined mares.

I have lost my tall boots, fur cloak, gold stirrups
and spurs.
My feet are sore and swollen with the wearing
of peasant's sandals
Made of plaited palm-leaves.
All my riches I gambled away for the sake of
frivolous amusement.
This, then, is my story;
This, by the same token, the story of the colored
knuckle-bones.

But — what can I do?
Not even Allah the One can turn a gambler
into a priest!
Not even Allah the One can turn a Moslem
into a Hindu,
Nor make him wear the thread of Brahmin
heathenry!

Thus Timoor Khan, the Waziri, sings.
The sweet-voiced ancient sings.
On the subject of himself and the colored
knuckle-bones
He says a few words.

Zomaun Khan, the Waziri...

◆

This ballad of the Afghan Waziris, commemorating a tribal fight with their southern neighbors, the Sharaunis, dates back to the middle of the eighteenth century when Ahmad Shah, the Afghan Amir of the Durani tribe, invaded India and defeated the army of Mohammed Shah, the Mogul emperor, and when all the border used this excuse for its national sport of raid and counter-raid. There exists an older ballad of the Balochis, rather similar in wording and spirit. In the original Pushtoo this ballad has an almost Homeric swing and epic rhythm which my English translation cannot render. (*From the border Afghan*)

◆

Zomaun Khan, the Waziri sings.
The honey-voiced poet sings.
The whirler of swords sings.
The son of Dowlut Khan sings.
Of the Waziris he sings with his tongue.
Of his own grand prowess he sings a few
words.

Send for the smith and bid him sharpen my
cheray of steel,
My snake-like blade of fine steel,
My jewel-flashing mistress of bright steel.
Sharpen it on the whirling stones.
For point and edge have been fasting too long.

Make six-nailed shoes for my slender mare.
Fasten the pointed nails with skilled fingers.
Saddle my dancing mare with my great
Bokharan saddle.

Give me rifle and knotted whip.
Give me my long black lance which bends like
a jointed sugar-cane.
For defying words have come to me from the
Sharaunis,
The wearers of lousy turbans.

59

The steel-wielding Sharaunis have trod the path
    of strife.
Back they are at the old sword trade.
They have dyed their stallions' manes red in
    sign of war.
They have planted a forest of threatening
    lances.
Led they are by Zoolfikhar Khan, the re-
    nowned,
The slayer of tigers,
The wide-stepping in battle.
Yet to me he is no more than an unripened
    turnip.
For can the power of the lamb rival the lion's
    might?

O Allah!
Grant me that tomorrow I may stop their
    gathered clansmen
In the sun-golden afternoon.

We will drop on them from the crest of the
    Suleymani hills.
Waziris will clash with Sharaunis.
We will pair off our gallant young warriors.
Jehan Khan will struggle with Achmed Naujib.
Amber-scented Mohammed Muddud will draw
    against Murad Khan.
Nusseer Khan will fight with mighty-thewed
    Nadir.
And I, with my black troop of wild asses,
Astride my slender mare, lance in hand,
Will search out and fight Zoolfikhar Khan.
And — Allah willing! — he will flee.
But I will pursue him on my slender mare.
Swiftly I will seize him by his lousy turban.
I will transfix him with sword and lance,
And my hand will be crimson with his blood.

Dead he will fall from his bay mare's saddle,
And he will sleep upon the plain,
While I give thanks to Allah, the One,
King of Daybreak.

Then, hereafter, I will carry off the women and
*   the cattle*
Of the dirty-robed Sharaunis,
In sign that I, Zomaun Khan, the Waziri,
Have slain Zoolfikhar Khan, the Sharauni,
And have folded about my forehead
The knotted, amber-scented turban of chieftain-
*   ship.*

Today, of the Afghans . . .

◆

This poem, of the late sixteenth century, belongs to the vast "literature of abuse" which has a distinct place in Central Asian poetry, and refers to the days when the Mogul emperors of Delhi, using bribery as often as soldiers, tried to subjugate Afghanistan. At first the Moguls succeeded, but later on, after long and disastrous warfare, they were forced to withdraw their troops to Hindustan. The Moguls had, in fact, the same experience as the British. The latter, too, to this day use bribery — though it is called "subsidies" in diplomatic parlance — to keep on the good side of the Afghans. The British, too, invaded the hills time and again. They, too, thanks to superior numbers and better war equipment, defeated the Afghans occasionally. They, too, ultimately, were always forced to return to Hindustan, leaving behind graves filled with Englishmen and Hindus — and nothing else. The last stanza of the poem is an allusion to those Afghans whom the Mogul emperor bribed successfully — if strictly temporarily — and therefore, as temporarily, called "loyal." (*From the northern Afghan*)

◆

*Today, of the Afghans once famed in the
    snow-clad hills,
    Are left the tribes of Mohmands,
    Bangashis, Warakzais, and Afridis.*

*The hounds of the Mohmands are better than
    the Bangashis,
Though the Mohmands themselves are worse
    than dogs.
The Warakzais are the scavenger-vultures of
    the Afridis,
Though all of them are only carrion-crows.*

*This is the truth about the best tribes of
    Afghans.
Allah! What then can I say of the worst?
In living Afghans is neither truth nor decency.
All good Afghans are dead and buried.*

Still — today of all Afghans the Mohmands
*   are best.*
This is a plain and simple fact to all who know
*   the hills.*

He to whom the Mogul emperor said: "You
*   are loyal to me,"*
Allah forbid that I should hide his stinking
*   shame!*
Let the Afghans drive all honor from their foul
*   souls.*
For they have been purchased by the Moguls'
*   red gold.*

There Came, Came There To Me ...

◆

The following Afghan love ballad, a *ghazal* in form, was written in the early nineteenth century by Pir Mohammed, a poet of Kabul, whose father was "*Ishikaghaussee*" or Master of the Outer Gate to Shah· Shuja, Amir of the Afghans. It has in the original Pushtoo a sweet, haunting cadence, largely due to the quaint arranging and repeating of words. I have tried to give a faint idea of it by giving, practically, a word for word translation. (*From the northern Afghan*)

◆

There came,
    Came there to me the hour of separation,
        Of separation came the hour.
My beloved plunged into my heart the red-hot
    iron of separation,
Of separation the red-hot iron.

Come not,
Come not to me, O doctor.
There are no drugs for mortal wound,
For mortal wound no drugs.
You cannot heal the red wound of separation,
Of separation the red wound.

There is none,
None there is to whom I can tell the tale of
        separation,
Of separation the tale.
Black and caked are the cinders of separation,
Of separation the cinders black and caked.

She was a branch of the sandalwood tree,
Of the sandalwood tree a branch.
She left me, and winter came,
Came winter.

Came the bleak, bleak storm of separation,
Of separation the bleak, bleak storm.

Fly away, O Pir Mohammed, from the tumult
    of the world,
From the world's tumult fly away.
For your little queen has put upon your brow
    the foot of separation,
Of separation the foot upon your brow.

The Most Fitting Subject...

◆

The miraculous account of the Creation of the Horse exists in many versions: Persian, Afghan, Tarantchi, Balochi, and others. The one which I am using I heard among the Tunganis, Tartars with a strong admixture of Chinese blood who have settled in Chinese Turkestan near the Thian-Shan mountains and, though strict Moslems, have largely adopted the Chinese language, their very name being derived from the Chinese *"tun-jen"* which means "military colonists." But, just as in the Highlands of Scotland some of the older people still remember legends and poems in the Gaelic, so, among the Tunganis, the older people have preserved some of their ancient tribal lore, such as the following, in the original, rather archaic Tartar tongue . . . a Tartar as different from the Tartar spoken, for instance, in the Crimea as Chaucerian English is different from the modern Chicago vulgate. In a way the Creation of the Horse is recitative prose — at least to the western ear. But the Oriental calls it poetry, accentuating the recitation with staccato drum beats, sudden pauses, and throaty, high-pitched yells. Underlying the obvious monotony of the tonal effect, a very sharp ear can even detect a distinct melody and rhythm — I mean, in the original. The *"Kalima,"* mentioned at the end of the poem, is the Moslem confession of faith. (*From the Tartar*)

◆

*T*he most fitting subject which the tongue of words should use with the using of tongue, is the exalted exalting of the Lord God's omnipotent omnipotence.

May His ninety-nine blessed names be praised!
May His ninety-nine praised names be blessed!

* * *

His is Creation, like a brocaded fabric, colored with exquisite designs and various groupings. He brought everything from nothing unto the basis of being.

66

May the Leavener of Clay be glorified!
May the Powerful Dispenser be glorified!

* * *

*Timoor Khan of pure progeny — may Allah
send him the delights of Paradise! — related
how God the Holder of the Scales of Justice
with the Strength of His Hands — may He be
exalted! — created the first man Adam Khan
— on him Peace! — out of clay, and from the
clay which remained in the mould in which
Adam Khan — on him Peace! — had been
shaped, the Lord God — may He be exalted!
— made seven things:*

       Dates;
       Grapes;
       Pomegranates;
       Steel;
       Women;
       Flowers;
   And, finally, the head of the horse.

* * *

*Then, out of His will, Allah — His All-Mercy
purifies the World! — created the Houris in
Paradise for the enjoyment of the righteous,
giving to them the secret of virginity that
eternally re-creates itself after each night of
passion. And from the saliva of the Houris —
may seven of them share my couch in the here-
after! — He created the horse's blood. And
from a splinter of His Seven-Stepped Throne of
Glory He fashioned the horse's body. And
from the blessed Tuba tree He made the horse's
mane. And then, with the polish and power of
His guiding will, He gave life to the whole.*

*   *   *

*Thus the Lord God — may He be exalted! —
made the horse most perfect of all created
things. And because of this the Messenger
Mohammed Mustaffa, the Seal of the Elected,
the Sweet Prophet, the Chief of the Mighty
Saints, the Great Apostle — on Him and His
Descendants the blessings of the One God! —
always kept his favorite horse by his side, and
was in the habit of cleaning its eyes and nostrils
with his own illustrious, green cloak and to give
it sweet barley to eat out of this same cloak.*

*   *   *

*This is the truth!
And it has also been said that sins are equal in
number to the hairs
Of the horse's mane.*

*   *   *

*Thus said the Khan Timoor Khan of pure
progeny,
The far-traveled Dervish.*

*   *   *

O Moslems, repeat the Kalima:
*"One the God is, and Mohammed is His
Messenger!"*

*   *   *

As the Ant Brought To Solomon . . .

◆

There are two main divisions of Afghan love poetry; that of the townspeople, the Heratis and Kabulis, which is filled "with the sound of swinging nose-rings and the glittering of *tikas* on the forehead of the beloved," and that of the Suleymani hillmen where the bazaar atmosphere gives way to the breeze of mountain and desert. But, though rare, there is a third class, in northern Afghanistan, where country, language, and people are more Turkoman than Afghan. Some of this poetry, due to the nearness and the cultural influence of the Middle Kingdom, is almost Chinese in its fleeting remoteness, its subtle, elusive charm. The following lines were written by captain Tcherkess Khan, an Afghan Turkoman who, in the middle of the last century, went north and served under Yakoob Khan when the latter using the title of *"Attalyk Ghazee"* or "Defender of the Faith," conquered Chinese Turkestan and dreamed great dreams of a huge Turkoman empire reaching from Pekin to Moscow, from the Crimea to Tibet. (*From the Turkoman*)

◆

*A*s the ant brought to Solomon the King
The thigh of a grass-hopper as an
offering,
So do I bring my soul, beloved, to thee.

*I have placed my head and my heart
On the sill of the door of my love.
Step gently, child!*

In the Hour of My Death . . .

◆

The following poem, to this day a favorite with the dancing girls and cour-
tezans of Kabul, was written in the late eighteenth century by Shikandar Khan
Tugluq who was *"Hirkarra-Bashee"* or chief of the intelligence department
to Shah Shuja, Amir of the Afghans, and who was on his father's side a "Sayyid,"
a direct descendant of the Prophet. He wrote the poem in Persian, then as
always the language of polite Central Asian society, and unintelligible, not only
in language but also in sentiment, to the great mass of Pushtoo-speaking popu-
lation. (*From the Persian*)

◆

*I*n the hour of my death, the Prophet — on
whom Peace! — will ask me:
'*What hast thou done, thou, my de-
scendant?*
*What hast thou done that is lasting and
splendid?*
What are thy claims to my blood and seed?
*By what right dost thou clamor at the door
of Paradise?*'

And I shall reply:
'*Peace on Thee, O Prophet of the One God!*
I have lied and I have cheated.
I have taken the name of God in vain.
*Twice I killed for passion, three times for
cruelty.*
I have sinned the many sins.
*Useless was my life, and stinking as hash-
eesh dregs.*
*But love came to me, O Prophet of the
One God.*
And I gave my all to her whom I loved.'

And I shall say:
'*For dearer she was to me than salvation,*
Dearer than honor,
Dearer than ambition and endeavor,

Dearer than ancient race and my pride of
clan,
Dearer than sun light and the light of the
moon,
Dearer than spring flowers and the breezes
of spring,
Dearer than summer gold and the ripeness of
summer,
Dearer than Thou, O Prophet of God — on
whom Peace!
And I gave to her my all — which was
little!'

In the hour of my death, the Prophet — on
whom Peace! — will ask me:
'What has thou done, thou, Shikandar
Khan Tugluq, my descendant?'
And I shall answer:
'I have loved her even as Thou — Peace on
Thee! — didst love Ayesha!
And I am of Thy blood and of Ayesha's
blood!'
And the Prophet — Peace on Him and the
Blessings of the One God! —
Will open wide the golden gates of Paradise
in the hour of my death, and will say:
'Enter, Shikandar Khan Tugluq, worthy of
my seed!'

In Every City I Seek Thee ...

◆

This poem was written, in the early seventeenth century, by Mullah Zukkee, a decidedly ungodly Moslem priest who founded, in Kabul, the esoteric Sufi lodge named after him. He was, incidentally, the author of a number of philosophical treatises which antedate Nietzsche's "Antichrist" by a brace of centuries. It is both comic and instructive to consider that the fair Zaida, whom he addresses in this poem, was the wife of an Uzbek nobleman from Tartary whom he killed and that, several years later, she was responsible for his death by having him — a historical fact — thrown into a cauldron of boiling mutton suet when he was drunk with Shirazi wine. The Shiite and Sunnite mentioned in this poem are the two main divisions of the Moslem religion. (*From the Persian*)

◆

In every city I seek thee, Zaida.
In every language I praise thee.
My heart holds thee, the one.

As the true believer seeks the truth of Allah
From mosque to mosque,
So, vainly, do I seek the like of thy face
From bazaar to bazaar.

I care not if thou be Shiite or Sunnite.
For Heresy and Orthodoxy stand both behind
The screen of thy beauty.

Orthodoxy to the Orthodox!
Heresy to the Heretic!
But to me, being a wise priest, the scent of thy
body,
The touch of thy mouth that sucks the soul
away!

Thy Passion Is the Scent . . .

◆

(The next poem, like the preceding, was written by Mullah Zukkee to his mistress Zaida. (*From the Persian*)

◆

Thy passion is the scent of the late-
blooming Kabul rose.
Thy anger is a thousand thorns.

Thus, for the sake of one rose, have I become
the slave
Of a thousand thorns.

A Gentleman Will Neither Eat Nor Rest...

◆

The following rather epic seventeenth century poem by Khushal Khan, chief and bard of the Khatak tribe of Afghans, needs little introduction. It is not only an extraordinary, if naïf, picture of the poet's personality, but gives also picturesque sidelights on the contemporary history, morals and customs of Afghanistan and Mogul India. (*From the southern Afghan*)

◆

*A gentleman will neither eat nor rest
Until he has avenged his wrongs upon
his enemy.
None will respect the man who does not respect
his own honor.
A slave who has honor and pride and intelligence
Is better than his lord who has less.
One cannot reach a mountain top at one leap.
The true man walks slowly, but steadily, upwards, always upwards.
Warily he walks, but without faltering,
And finds, at the end, the elixir of life.
Days differ. One day brings pain; another
cures.
But honor never changes.
What is within another's reach you, too, can
reach,
Be you a gentleman.
For a gentleman holds the reins of his own fate
and fancy.*

*He whose ancestors hewed out dominion with
the sword,
Let him take up this sword. To wield it is his
trade.*

74

My son Abad Khan is brave and victorious.
He has upheld my honor and renewed the glory
of my name.
May Allah grant that he rival me in living
and doing.
Let his enemies, if they be wise, beware of him.
For his sword is a cobra, eager for blood.
May my other sons follow Abad Khan and
obey him.
For war is a difficult trade.   Only one man can
be leader.

A gentleman is generous with gifts and food.
The tiger is content with the blue bull's neck,
And leaves the rest to jackal and to fox.
A single Afghan hound kills the great stag of
the plains.
While yelping curs nose the village dung heaps.

I was defeated at Ganbut; but at Doda I was
victorious.
High on a mountain peak, the Fort of Doda
was hard to take.
It was stronger than the Fort of Kohat, with
seven outer walls.
But, with Allah's help, my son Abad Khan
conquered it in two days.
Great was the slaughter.   Our swords bloomed
like red flowers.
Far down the valley clashed the echo of
Bahram's blade.
Amongst the slain the rifle smoke rose gray and
thick,
Vaulting an eighth heaven above Allah's seven
heavens.
The spears of my Khataks pierced the enemies'
armor
As a bazaar tailor runs his needle through cloth.

The lance-wielders of my Khataks
Vanquished the tough, red-faced riders of the
    Bangash.
There was a great deal of body to body fighting,
Nor was there lack of arrows and snake-like
    daggers.
Sadar Khan is my youngest son, fifteen years
    of age.
Never before had he seen a battle.
But on that day he dyed his spear scarlet with
    blood,
Until my grief at the defeat at Ganbut left
    my soul.
A great stench rose from the heaps of slain
Whom our whirling swords cut to pieces at
    Doda.
We drove the surviving Bangash up to the
    peaks of Pali.
Let them now hide their blades within their
    scabbards.

Their lives no greater fool than he
Who leaves his own trade for another's.
A stag is fierce when the hound attacks him,
But the tiger kills him at one blow.
I would not have cut down a single almond tree
    in their gardens,
Had the Bangash been honorable gentlemen.
But they were dishonorable, and I punished
    them.
Now the little jackals are feasting on their flesh.
Such is the proper punishment for the slave
Who quarrels with his master.

At the Fort of Doda we once more filled the
    goblet
Which our defeat at Ganbut had emptied.
On that day we took enormous plunder:

Lovely women, splendid stallions, and fine
  jewels.
There was not a Khatak warrior who did not
  fit himself out
With the weapons and black armor of the
  Bangash.
There were six or seven thousand Khataks
  in that fight,
And all thanked Allah for their share of the
  loot.

The glory of this battle will spread throughout
  the land,
And every Afghan will be proud of us.
But when the rumor of it reaches Hindustan,
The Mogul emperor will tremble with rage.
For such a King in Islam is Aurungzeb
That only Afghan disgrace can cause him joy.

In the change from the constellation of the Lion,
In the year 1091 of the Hegira, in the month
  of Rajah,
On the third day after the fight of Doda, I
  began this poem.
Deeds recorded on paper remain for posterity
  to read.
That is why I wrote down the tale of this battle.

May my sons be always as victorious over their
  enemies
As Khushal Khan was on that day — Allah
  be praised!

They Say: Dost Mohammed, the Ghazi...

◆

In the third decade of the nineteenth century the youngest of the famous twelve Barukzai brothers, Dost Mohammed Khan, of the Durani clan, made himself Amir of the Afghans. Afraid of the growing strength of the Sikh nation under their ruler, Ranjit Singh, he proclaimed Holy War, and from all Central Asia the Moslem warriors, Tartars, Tarantchis, Kirgiz, Bokharans, Karakalpaks, Turkomans, and the Russian, Chinese, and Siberian Moslems flocked to his banners. Ranjit Singh, a clever diplomat, sent Harlan, an American adventurer, to Peshawar where the latter succeeded in sowing the seeds of dissension amongst the Barukzai brothers and persuading one of them, Sultan Mohammed, to desert with his troops. The poem, by Achmed Gul, refers to a minor battle between the Afghans under Mohammed Akbar, Dost Mohammed's son, and the Sikhs under Hari Singh. To explain certain allusions: *"Ghazi"* means "Fanatic" — but in the honorable, not the opprobrious sense of the word. The *"Kalima"* is the Moslem confession of faith: "One the God is, and Mohammed is His Messenger." The penultimate stanza means that Achmed Gul, the poet, did not consider himself sufficiently well paid for having written the poem. (*From the northern Afghan*)

◆

They say:
Dost Mohammed, the Ghazi, makes
ready for war at Kabul.
Loud is the crackle of steel in Kandahar,
the King's town.

They say:
Dost Mohammed, the Amir, has chosen the
path of strife.
He has proclaimed Holy War. He is lead-
ing his young warriors.
Grant them victory, O Allah!

Shamelessly the enemies ran away when Mo-
hammed Akbar attacked them.

O Khan, be firm in the faith of Islam!
The Kalima will be your dagger and
shield.

They say:
Dost Mohammed, the Ghazi, makes ready
for war at Kabul.
He fights quick rear-guard actions,
He has mounted his light artillery on
camels.
Loud is the crackle of steel in Kandahar,
the King's town.

* * *

He has given battle to the Sikhs,
The eaters of dirt.
The soldiers of the Ghazi Amir are off to the
red war.

The rifle bullets drop like hail.
The Ghazis give their heads to Allah.
They are Duranis, strong and mighty.

Hari Singh was the proudest of the
Sikhs.
But defeat enveloped him like a dun
cloud.
The Ghazis cut the heathen into carrion,
They cut them to pieces with their shining,
snake-like swords.

They say:
Dost Mohammed, the Ghazi, makes ready
for war at Kabul.
The martyrs bloom like red flowers.
Loud is the crackle of steel in Kandahar,
the King's town.

* * *

*Hari Singh has written a letter and sent it
to Ranjit Singh:*
*"Hurry to the rescue. The Sikhs are re-
treating toward Panjtar."*

*The Ghazis — have they not come from
all the Moslem lands?*
Pray to God.
They have come to battle for Islam.
They have arrived before Peshawar.

*When they drew their slender Egyptian blades,
lightning flashed silver.*
The Sikhs ran away,
Their scalp locks flying in the wind.

They say:
Dost Mohammed, the Ghazi, makes ready
for war at Kabul.
O Khan, we have dyed the manes of our
stallions crimson in sign of war.
Loud is the crackle of steel in Kandahar,
the King's town.

* * *

Sikhs and Ghazis clashed in battle.
*The Sikhs vanished before the attack of
the Ghazis.*
*The survivors took refuge in the brittle
desert.*

*My spiritual master at Paimal is a saintly
priest.*
I am Achmed Gul.
*I came, and all the other poets trembled with
envy.*
*O, had Allah only granted that I, too, might
have fought in this Holy War!*

Today Achmed Gul is furious,
Thief! Jackal! Away! Away!

They say:
Dost Mohammed, the Ghazi, makes ready
for war at Kabul.
Loud is the crackle of steel in Kandahar,
the King's town.

Dost Mohammed Said...

◆

This is an anonymous ballad and, like the preceding, deals with the Holy War between Dost Mohammed Khan and the Sikhs under Ranjit Singh. Sher Singh, mentioned in the poem, was a famous Sikh general and Fath Khan an Afghan hero. "Singh" after a name designates a Sikh, and by changing Sultan Mohammed to Sultan Singh, the anonymous poet effectively describes his treachery, just as during the World War a pro-German Scot might have been labeled as "Herr Macdonald." (*From the northern Afghan*)

◆

Dost Mohammed said:
Allah, Thou art the protector of hundreds
of thousands by Thy great might.
I shall fight the Sikhs with my fifty thousand
wielders of snake-like swords.
Our fame will grow greatly.
But the reckoning of the Sikh cowards is yet
to come."

Dost Mohammed, the Ghazi, is a master of
sword in battle.
He is a reckless man at sword-time.
He is a keen gambler at sword-play.
He has girt on his Persian weapons.
Mounted on his chestnut stallion,
He is the devourer of his foes.

Dost Mohammed said:
"I am going to war. I am a martyr.
I am going on Crusade.
With clean heart I shall fight for the honor of
Islam.
I shall drive Sher Singh to the lowlands.
I shall invade the lands of the English
And plunder Amritsar and all the Punjab."

Came warriors from Amritsar, Lahore, and all
the Punjab.
Here, everywhere, are now the heathen warriors.
May all the cursed Hindu unbelievers burn in
hell fire in the hereafter!
From Kandahar came our young men, our
handsome soldiers,
To chase them away.
Our young men came from Kandahar. At
Shaykhan they made camp.
But they lost their chance.
They did not attack the Sikhs.
Allah's curse on all the Sirdars!
May they be homeless, driven like beggars
from door to door,
Until the Day of Resurrection!

May their faces be black until the Day of
Resurrection!
Lying Sirdars!
Without fighting, you abandoned your land to
the Sikhs, O Sultan Mohammed!
Your shroud is your armor, O Sirdar!
Why, O dog, did you not defend the
Kaibar Pass?

I am speaking the truth about the Sirdars from
my own mind.
They are pigs, stealing grain from the horse's
nose bag.
They are cowards.
The arrows of war pierce them from the back
In the fatter spots of their hind parts.

The Sirdars deserted, forcing Dost Mohammed,
the Ghazi, to retreat before
The enemy.

83

The Barukzai, Sultan Mohammed, has denied
God.
Sayyid Mohammed, Pir Mohammed and his
son Hassan have disappeared.
O Khan, why did you not send out swift riders
mounted on camels
And commanded by Mohammed Akbar to
guard against treachery?

The Sirdars deserted, and Dost Mohammed
Khan's great army was helpless.
Akbar Khan was clad in shining silver armor.
The Khan Jamah Khan defended the rear.
Came famous Fath Khan, the man of noble
heart, to lend his help.

Fath Khan came from Panjtar.
Great was his courage.
There were also the Khan Hajji Khan and
Jamah Khan, handsome as a flower,
And all the beautiful, black-haired young nobles
of the Duranis.
Yar Khan came, the bright lamp of sorrowful
eyes,
And Abdullah Khan, the reliever of oppression.
Allah bless all the Duranis!
They are of the Prophet's seed!

They came to go on Crusade, all the young
warriors of Bunir,
And the Eusufzyes, the Mohmandzyes, and the
men from the eight towns.
They struck with the bright swords.
But the Sirdars deserted.
They spoke falsely to chiefs and generous lords,
To gentlemen and rulers of forts.

There was great steel clash when Eusufzyes
and Mohmandzyes rushed into fight.
Ranjit Singh trembled and said:
"This is the song of the sword of the Sahib
of Sowatt!"
But Sultan Singh was a traitor to Dost
Mohammed.
One by one the Ghazis died on the field of battle.